Family Math Night:

Math Standards in Action

Jennifer Taylor-Cox, Ph.D.

EYE ON EDUCATION
6 DEPOT WAY WEST, SUITE 106
LARCHMONT, NY 10538
(914) 833-0551
(914) 833-0761 fax
www.eyeoneducation.com

Library of Congress Cataloging-in-Publication Data

Taylor-Cox, Jennifer.
Family math night : math standards in action / Jennifer Taylor-Cox.
    p. cm.
ISBN 1-930556-99-3
1. Mathematics--Study and teaching (Elementary)--Activity programs.
2. Education--Parent participation.   I. Title.
QA135.6.T35 2005
372.7--dc22   2004030219

Book design services provided by
Jennifer Osterhouse Graphic Design
3752 Danube Drive, Davidsonville, MD 21035
(410-798-8585)

Also available from Eye On Education

**A Collection of Performance Tasks and Rubrics:
Primary School Mathematics**
Charlotte Danielson and Pia Hansen Powell

**A Collection of Performance Tasks and Rubrics:
Upper Elementary School Mathematics**
Charlotte Danielson

**A Collection of Performance Tasks and Rubrics:
Middle School Mathematics**
Charlotte Danielson

**A Collection of Performance Tasks and Rubrics:
High School Mathematics**
Charlotte Danielson and Elizabeth Marquez

**Bringing the NCTM Standards to Life:
Best Practices for Middle Schools**
Yvelyne Germain-McCarthy

**Bringing the NCTM Standards to Life:
Exemplary Practices from High Schools**
Yvelyne Germain-McCarthy

**Mathematics and Multi-Ethnic Students:
Exemplary Practices**
Yvelyne Germain-McCarthy & Katharine Owens

Teaching Mathematics in the Block
Susan Gilkey and Carla Hunt

**Assessment in Middle and High School Mathematics:
A Teacher's Guide**
Daniel Brahier

About the Author

Dr. Jennifer Taylor-Cox is an energetic, captivating presenter and well-known educator. She is the Executive Director of **Innovative Instruction: Connecting Research and Practice in Education**. Jennifer serves as an educational consultant for numerous districts across the United States. Her workshops and keynote speeches are always high-energy and insightful. She earned her Ph.D. from the University of Maryland and was awarded the "Outstanding Doctoral Research Award" from the University of Maryland and the "Excellence in Teacher Education Award" from Towson University. She currently serves as the president-elect of the Maryland Council of Teachers of Mathematics. Jennifer truly understands how to connect research and practice in education. Her passion for mathematics education is alive in her work with students, parents, teachers, and administrators.

Dr. Taylor-Cox lives and has her office in Severna Park, Maryland. She is the mother of three children.

If you would like to have Dr. Taylor-Cox present on Family Math Night at your school or if you would like to schedule professional development opportunities for educators and/or parents, please contact her at **Innovative Instruction: Connecting Research and Practice in Education**.

Jennifer Taylor-Cox, Ph.D., Educational Consultant
Office: 410-729-5599, Fax: 410-729-3211
Email: Jennifer@Taylor-CoxInstruction.com

Acknowledgments

In memory of Melvin Ortiz.

Appreciation is extended to my friend and colleague, Christine Oberdorf, an exemplary mathematics educator and outstanding implementer of many Family Math Nights.

Gratitude is expressed to Karren Schultz-Ferrell, early childhood mathematics expert and Michael Cox, dedicated pre-service teacher.

Special thanks to other reviewers Melissa Freiberg, Sharon O'Meallie, and Andrea LaChance.

Extensive acknowledgment and gratitude are offered to the thousands of students and parents who have taken part in my Family Math Night activities over the years.

Jennifer Taylor-Cox

Jennifer Osterhouse, Book Design

Marida Hines, Illustration

Table of Contents

Chapter One: Introduction 1

Why Should Our School Have Family Math Night?.....................1

How is *Family Math Night: Math Standards in Action* Organized?...2

How are the Activities Connected to Math Standards? 3

Why Should We Use Manipulatives in Mathematics?..................5

Why is "Questions Parents Can Ask" Included? 6

Why is There a Challenge for Each Activity? 6

What are Some Additional Tips for a Successful Family Math Night?...6

What is the Teacher's Role during Family Math Night? 8

Chapter Two: Primary Stations
(Prekindergarten Through Second Grade)............................9

Try to Go Home 10

Is It More or Less? 12

Let's Shake It Up! 14

Frog Hop Addition 16

Towers 18

Let's Go to the Bank 20

The Doorbell Rang Again 22

Pasta Patterns 24

Make It Balanced 26

Where's the Penny? 28

Tangrams 30

Geoboard Shapes 32

My Shoes 34

How Much Will It Hold? 36

Graphing Color Cubes 38

Chapter Three: Intermediate Stations
(Third Through Fifth Grades) 41

Magic Squares...42

Which Place is Best?...44

Hooray Array..46

Multiply on the Fly 48

Money Toss 50

Money is the Key 52

Clothesline Fractions..54

Fruit Salad 56

A Handful of Handshakes 58

Fun with the Greedy Triangle 60

Geo Goes Home 62

The Curse of Measurement 64

Honeybees 66

Pentominoes 68

My Spinners 70

Chapter Four: General Stations
(Prekindergarten Through Fifth Grade) **73**

Let's Build Odd & Even Sums 74

Cereal Chains 76

Mancala is an Old Favorite 78

Can Family 80

Pattern Block Pictures 82

Just a Minute 84

How Long for a Kiss? 86

Red Hot and Ice Cold 88

Bubbles Bubbles 90

Don't Pig Out 92

Chapter Five: Additional Tools **95**

Family Math Night Invitation to Parents 96

Family Math Night Journal Cover 97

Family Math Night Evaluation Form 98

Try to Go Home 99

Let's Go to the Bank 100

Tangrams 101

Graphing Color Cubes 103

Which Place is Best? 104

Money Toss 105

Money is the Key 106

Fruit Salad 108

Geo Goes Home 109

Pentominoes 111

My Spinners 112

Pattern Block Pictures 113

Just a Minute 114

Permission is granted to photocopy the pages in this book for your school's Family Math Night.

Chapter One:
Introduction

Why Should Our School Have Family Math Night?

The goal of Family Math Night is to strengthen the mathematical aptitudes of students through the power of family interaction. By sponsoring Family Math Night, educators are encouraging parents and students to appreciate the energy and pleasure of mathematics. Each activity is designed to promote mathematical thinking and communication. The hands-on approach presented in this book helps make learning mathematics a meaningful and productive process for all involved.

Parents play an important role in the academic lives of students. By participating in Family Math Night, parents can serve as models of motivation, persistence, and competency to their children. The directions for each activity are presented in a clear, concise manner,

allowing parents to guide students to more complete understandings of various mathematics concepts. At the same time, parents may be learning new knowledge and solidifying or revising previous knowledge about mathematics. You may hear parents saying, "I never really understood that concept until I tried this activity with my child," or "I never knew math could be so fun!" In many ways, the Family Math Night activities enlighten parents as they begin to understand and value mathematics in new ways.

The concepts presented in each Family Math Night activity will help students learn essential new skills and/or reinforce skills already learned in mathematics. While working through math problems in a textbook is one way for some students to learn mathematics, there are other more interactive means of gaining knowledge of mathematics, such as the math stations presented in this book. To help realize a vision of increased math proficiency for all, we need to encourage students to think about and apply mathematics in the real world. Family Math Night can help students become mathematically fulfilled and empowered!

How is *Family Math Night: Math Standards in Action* Organized?

Family Math Night: Math Standards in Action contains five chapters. The first chapter addresses the goals and intentions of this book. The second chapter presents fifteen math stations for primary students (prekindergarten through second grade). The third chapter offers fifteen math stations for intermediate students (third through fifth grades). The fourth chapter presents ten more math stations designed for all students (prekindergarten through fifth grade). The final chapter provides additional tools for the successful implementation of Family Math Night.

There are two pages for each math station. The first page offers a list of the materials needed for the station, helpful hints, and math standards in action. The second page offers the directions, questions parents can ask, and a challenge. The first page is for educators to review and use to prepare each station. The second page can be photocopied and displayed at the Family Math Night station. The directions page can be laminated and mounted. Some educators find it helpful to attach each direction sheet to a file folder. The opened folder can be placed vertically at each station. Other educators prefer to place the direction sheets into display stands or onto display boards. In either case, the point is to have the directions clearly displayed at each station.

How are the Activities Connected to Math Standards?

Each Family Math Night station highlights a specific mathematics strand of the curriculum. The math connections given for each activity align with the *National Council of Teachers of Mathematics Principles and Standards* (NCTM, 2000). One of the unique features of this book is the border around each activity page. There are five distinct borders that correlate with the five math content strands. The standards include number and operations, algebra, geometry, measurement, and data analysis and probability.

Number and operations

Number and operations is a strand of the curriculum that promotes the understanding of numbers; number relationships; and the operations of addition, subtraction, multiplication, and division. The focus is on helping students develop number sense and computational proficiency.

Algebra

Algebra is a strand of the curriculum that highlights patterns, relationships, equality, functions, and models of representing math situations. The focus is on helping students recognize mathematical relationships, solve for unknowns, and establish ways of understanding and representing mathematics.

Geometry

Geometry is a strand of the curriculum that emphasizes the characteristics and properties of shape, spatial relationships, and visual representations. The focus is on encouraging students to utilize and strengthen skills in visualization, spatial reasoning, and geometric representations.

Measurement

Measurement is a strand of the curriculum that underscores the importance of understanding how objects are measured. Considering and experiencing appropriate units, processes, and tools are essential aspects of learning measurement.

Data analysis and probability

Data analysis and probability comprise the strand of the curriculum that highlights statistical information and the concepts associated with the likelihood of outcomes. It is important for students to understand how to collect, organize, analyze, and interpret data and to understand fundamental concepts of probability.

The Family Math Night stations are also connected to the NCTM (2000) process standards. These standards include problem solving, reasoning and proof, communication, connections, and representations. Problem solving is present in many of the activities as students and parents work together to reach solutions using knowledge and experience in mathematics. Reasoning and proof are associated with providing evidence of mathematical conjectures. As students explain and justify processes and answers, they are offering the reasoning and proof associated with sound mathematics. Communication is emphasized in the activities as students discuss and record their mathematical ideas and thinking processes. Connections are established as students come to understand how math ideas are related to each other and to the real world. Representations are given emphasis in the ways in which students model, organize, discuss, and record the mathematics associated with each activity.

Why Should We Use Manipulatives in Mathematics?

Using manipulatives in mathematics allows students to experience abstract concepts in a concrete manner. Building models to represent math ideas and concepts strengthens the conceptual frameworks students construct as they apply math to everyday life. Manipulatives provide the means by which many students need to express the reasoning and evidence associated with the math thinking. Using manipulatives to show how one derives an answer helps solidify understanding. Manipulatives offer students the tools to solve mathematical situations. Additionally, manipulatives often serve as the springboard for math communication as students explain and justify how they solve a problem and/or approach a solution.

To encourage the successful use of math manipulatives, educators should think about how the manipulatives are organized and how they are made available to students. For example, sets of manipulatives can be prepared and stored in plastic bags, baskets, or other containers. The listed manipulatives must be made available to students and parents at each Family Math Night station.

Why is "Questions Parents Can Ask" Included?

Asking questions invites students to engage in mathematical communication. Questions promote mathematical thinking and encourage "math talk." We do not want the Family Math Night room to be a "quiet zone." Instead, we want to strive for a room full of active mathematics participants who are engaged in productive mathematics dialogue. By promoting "math talk" at Family Math Night, we will better prepare our students for the mathematical challenges ahead. Our role is to provide students with opportunities to hear, use, and come to know the richness of "math talk."

Why is There a Challenge for Each Activity?

Purposeful challenge serves to inspire and enlighten many students. Each Family Math Night activity includes a challenge that provides a possible extension of the activity. Sometimes students are so engaged in the activity that they want to investigate it further. Other times students go directly to the challenge as a way to increase the level of difficulty. Essentially, the challenges offer a way to differentiate the learning opportunities for children and their families.

What are Some Additional Tips for a Successful Family Math Night?

If you want high attendance at your Family Math Night, you need to advertise to students and the parents. Send home notices about the event (a sample notice to parents is found on page 96). Include the event in newsletters and on the school calendar. Offer incentives for students and parents. Some schools offer recognition to the class with the highest attendance. Other schools encourage students to attend by allowing participation in Family Math Night to serve as the night's homework. The possibilities are endless!

To accommodate many families you will need a large room or several large rooms. Position the tables in a manner that allows for maximum movement and comfort. Posting multiple copies of the directions and providing several sets of the materials allow you to have more than one family at each Family Math Night station. Also, color-coding the directions pages can be very helpful. For example, all of the primary activities can be photocopied on yellow paper, all of the intermediate stations can be photocopied on blue paper, and all of the general activities can be photocopied on green paper. This coding system helps parents direct their children toward grade-level appropriate activities. If you decide to color-code the activities, provide parents with a key indicating the coding system upon entry.

Providing a check-in table is a good idea. Parents can sign in students or teachers can check off students on class lists. The check-in area is a place where students can obtain pencils and Family Math Night journals. The journals can be simple booklets of blank pages for students to record information related to the activities. A sample Family Math Night journal cover is found on page 97. Evaluation forms can also be distributed at the check-in area. A sample Family Math Night evaluation form is found on page 98. The information gathered from the evaluations will help you plan subsequent Family Math Nights.

What is the Teacher's Role During Family Math Night?

During Family Math Night, educators should highlight the mathematical endeavors of students and parents. While visiting families at each station, educators should also encourage math conversation and math thinking. Some of the consumable materials may need to be replenished, and some of the stations need to be monitored. However, be sure to take at least one moment during Family Math Night to notice how the event mathematically inspires and empowers students and parents!

Chapter Two:
Primary Stations

(Prekindergarten Through Second Grade)

Try to Go Home

Is It More or Less?

Let's Shake It Up!

Frog Hop Addition

Towers

Let's Go to the Bank

The Doorbell Rang Again

Pasta Patterns

Make It Balanced

Where's the Penny?

Tangrams

Geoboard Shapes

My Shoes

How Much Will It Hold?

Graphing Color Cubes

Try to Go Home

Materials:

    Game board (see page 99)
    Marker (pawn, chip, or other counter)
    Number cube (die)

Helpful Hints:

Sometimes participants try to play this game with two markers. Remind participants that they are sharing one marker in this activity.

Math Standards in Action:

Try to Go Home is an activity that reinforces one-to-one correspondence for young students. Students count the number of dots shown on the number cube and count that number of spaces to move on the board. By actively taking part in many experiences with one-to-one correspondence, young students build important foundations in understanding and representing numbers.

Try to Go Home

Directions:

1. Place one marker on the center spot of the game board.

2. The first (youngest) player rolls the number cube and moves toward her/his "Home" spot.

3. The second player rolls the number cube and moves using the same marker toward her/his "Home" spot.

4. Play continues until a player reaches her/his "Home" spot.

Questions Parents Can Ask:

Who is closer to the "Home" spot?

How many more spaces do you need to go?

How likely is it to roll a six?

Challenge:

Try using the sum of two number cubes to find the number of spaces to move each turn.

Is It More or Less?

Materials:

Deck of playing cards (without face cards)

Helpful Hints:

Use cards that have numbers that are easy to read.

Math Standards in Action:

Is It More or Less? is an activity that encourages students to understand the relative position and magnitude of whole numbers. By stating whether a number is more than, less than, or equal to another number, students are gaining experiences that help to develop number sense. Specifically, students are engaging in early explorations of the relationships among numbers by using numeric expressions.

Is It More or Less?

Directions:

1. Each player chooses one card and displays it.

2. Players say the more than, less than, or equal to statement. For example, "Seven is more than five."

3. The player who has the greater number takes both cards.

4. If the cards are equal, each player keeps her/his own card.

5. Continue playing through the deck. The winner is the player with the most cards.

Questions Parents Can Ask:

Which card is less than the other card?

How much more is the greater number?

How close are the cards to being equal?

Challenge:

Choose two cards and add the numbers together.

Let's Shake It Up!

Materials:

Beans painted blue on one side
(or two-colored counters)
Cans (film canisters or small cups)

Helpful Hints:

Paint large lima beans prior to Family Math Night. When painting, spread beans out on paper or in a large cardboard box. Use non-toxic spray paint (blue) to coat only one side of the beans. Allow painted beans to dry in a well-ventilated area.

Math Standards in Action:

Let's Shake It Up! is an activity that allows students to build foundations in numbers and operations. Students are exploring with number values and the meaning of the operation of addition. Specifically, students are working with a concept often referred to as "part-part-whole." Part of the whole (total) is represented with blue beans, and part of the whole (total) is represented with white beans. Understanding that a given total can be represented by different parts is a critical aspect of working with numbers and operations.

Let's Shake It Up!

Directions:

1. Count the total number of beans in the can.

2. Shake up the can of beans and pour them out.

3. Count the number of beans showing the blue side.

4. Count the number of beans showing the white side.

5. Record the blue + white addition sentence (equation) in your math journal.

6. Continue shaking, pouring, counting, and recording.

Questions Parents Can Ask:

If you know the total and the number of blue beans, do you know the number of white beans without counting them?

How many different combinations are there to show the total number of beans?

Challenge:

Change the total number of beans and play again.

Try this activity using subtraction ideas.

Frog Hop Addition

Materials:

Small plastic frogs
Number lines (0 to 10, 0 to 20, 0 to 30)
Number cubes (dice)

Helpful Hints:

If possible, laminate the number lines prior to
Family Math Night.

If available, use different colored frogs and/or
number lines.

Math Standards in Action:

Frog Hop Addition encourages students to utilize
an addition strategy known as "counting on."
This strategy is one of the basic addition strategies
employed by young students. Additionally, using the
number line to add numbers is a practice that helps
to build fluency with number sequence and number
relationships.

Frog Hop Addition

Directions:

1. Choose a frog.

2. Roll the number cube.

3. Place the frog on that number on the number line.

4. Roll the number cube again.

5. Make the frog hop to the right on the number line as many times as is shown on the number cube.

6. Write the addition sentence (equation) in your math journal: start + hop = stop

Questions Parents Can Ask:

*Where did the frog stop?

*How many hops would it take for your frog to get to ten/twenty/thirty?

Challenge:

Try a two hop addition sentence:
start + hop + hop = stop

Towers

Materials:

Connecting cubes
  (snap cubes, unifix cubes, or multilinks)
Stopwatch

Helpful Hints:

Use cubes that easily connect together to form a stack (tower).

Depending on the brand of the stopwatch, directions for how to "reset" may need to be available.

Math Standards in Action:

The *Towers* activity encourages students to work with numbers and operations. By participating in experiences associated with counting on and counting back, students begin to understand the results of adding and subtracting whole numbers. Likewise, students are developing number sense as they compose (put together) and decompose (break apart) various whole numbers.

Towers

Directions:

1. Use a stopwatch to keep time.

2. Connect the cubes to build a tower of one color.

3. Stop building at one minute.

4. Add to your tower using a different color for fifteen seconds. Or take away from your tower for fifteen seconds.

5. Use a counting on or a counting back strategy to solve the addition/subtraction situation.

6. Write the addition/subtraction sentence in your math journal.

Questions Parents Can Ask:

If you put the largest number in your head, can you count on/back in your mind?

What if you had two minutes to build?

Challenge:

Try building with your eyes closed or while standing on one foot or with one hand.

Let's Go to the Bank

Materials:

"Check" template (see page 100)
Play cash register
Play bills and coins

Helpful Hints:

The majority of coins should be pennies, nickels, and dimes, but quarters and half-dollars should also be available.

The majority of the bills should be ones, fives, and tens, but larger bills should also be available.

Multiple copies of "checks" should be available.

Math Standards in Action:

Let's Go to the Bank enables students to apply knowledge of numbers and number values. The acts of writing a check and cashing the amount allow students to connect number words, symbols, and quantities. Working with money encourages meaningful practice with the base 10 number system.

Let's Go to the Bank

Directions:

1. Write yourself a check for any amount less than twenty dollars.

2. Record the amount of money in your math journal.

3. Deposit your check in the cash register.

4. Count out the correct amount of money.

Questions Parents Can Ask:

Which coins/bills did you use?

Could you show the same amount of money using different coins/bills?

What if you had one dollar less?

Challenge:

Try making change for coins and bills.

The Doorbell Rang Again

Materials:

The Doorbell Rang by Pat Hutchins
Counters

Helpful Hints:

Provide several copies of the book.

Try to use counters that resemble cookies.

Math Standards in Action:

The Doorbell Rang Again is an activity that allows students to work with real-life applications of numbers and operations. The story encourages students to understand situations that call for division and fractional parts of a set. Through the meaningful use of manipulatives, young children gain knowledge in equal grouping and fair sharing.

The Doorbell Rang Again

Directions:

1. Read *The Doorbell Rang* by Pat Hutchins.

2. Use counters to represent the cookies and retell/demonstrate the story.

3. Write or draw part of the story in your math journal.

Questions Parents Can Ask:

How many cookies for each person? How do you know?

What if the doorbell rang only one time in the story?

What if there were twice as many cookies in the story?

What patterns do you notice?

Challenge:

Try making up your own story about division and fractions.

Pasta Patterns

Materials:

Various shapes/types of colored pasta (uncooked)

Helpful Hints:

Pasta needs to be colored prior to Family Math Night. Pasta can be colored using food coloring and rubbing alcohol. Mix several drops of food coloring with rubbing alcohol. Stir pasta in the colored rubbing alcohol until the desired shade is reached (several minutes). Remove pasta from liquid and allow to dry overnight.

Math Standards in Action:

The *Pasta Patterns* activity provides young students with an opportunity to work with understanding patterns, which is one of the key elements of algebraic thinking. Understanding patterns, relations, and functions begins with the identification of repeating and growing patterns. While repeating patterns have terms that repeat, growing patterns have terms that are based on a constant change. When students describe, expand, and create repeating and growing patterns they strengthen their ability to think algebraically.

Pasta Patterns

Directions:

1. **Make a repeating pattern using the pasta.
   For example, straight, straight, curly, straight,
   straight, curly, . . .**

2. **See if your partner can describe the repeating part
   of the pattern.**

3. **Make a growing pattern with the pasta.
   For example, 2, 4, 6, 8, . . .**

4. **See if your partner can tell what comes next.**

Questions Parents Can Ask:

What comes next? How do you know?

How many different items are in the pattern?

Can you make a pattern that does not consider color?

Challenge:

**Try making a circular repeating pattern, allowing
the repeating pattern to be continuous.**

Make It Balanced

Materials:

Snap cubes, unifix cubes, or multilinks
Two-pan balance

Helpful Hints:

Connect a few cubes together in various combinations and orientations for students to use as possible models.

This activity works best if cubes are centered at equal distances from the center of the balance.

Math Standards in Action:

Make It Balanced is an activity designed to highlight equality, which is one of the cornerstone concepts of algebra. To understand how to represent and analyze numeric structures, young students need to strengthen their knowledge of equality. This activity allows students to use concrete objects to represent values in an equation. When investigating which value is needed to balance the pans, students are engaging in early ways to solve for unknowns. The activity is also connected to measurement of weight.

Make It Balanced

Directions:

1. **Connect cubes together to form various values. Create groups of two, three, four, five, and six.**

2. **Place two groups on one side of the scale. For example, 3 + 4 on one side of the balance.**

3. **Place one group on the other side of the balance. For example, 5 on the other side of the balance.**

4. **Find out which value is needed to "make it balanced." Encourage students to count and estimate to create a balanced equation. For the above example, students find 3 + 4 = 5 + 2.**

   Note: Consider the arrangement of the cubes when creating a balanced equation. To accurately portray the equation on a two-pan balance, the cubes must be placed at equal distances from the center of the balance.

5. **Record some of the equations in your math journal.**

Questions Parents Can Ask:

Which value do we need to make it balanced?

Is there another way to make the sides equal?

Challenge:

Try larger number values.

Where's the Penny?

Materials:

Pennies
Ten small cups
Extra cups for the challenge

Helpful Hints:

Label the cups 1 to 10. Make sure you can read the labels when the cups are upside down.

Label extra cups (11-20) for the challenge.

Math Standards in Action:

Where's the Penny? invites young students to explore ideas of early geometry as they work with relative positions. By using words such as before, after, higher, and lower, students are applying what they know about how positions are defined and related. When students use these position words, they are uncovering important elements of geometry and number relationships.

Where's the Penny?

Directions:

1. One person hides the penny under one of the ten cups.

2. The other person tries to guess where the penny is "hiding."

3. Clues such as "before," "after," "higher," and "lower" are given.

4. Each time a guess is made, talk about which cups can be eliminated.

5. Try to guess where the penny is "hiding" using the least number of guesses.

Questions Parents Can Ask:

Do you know where the penny is __not__ hiding?

Where could the penny be now?

Which questions helped you the most? Why?

Challenge:

Try this activity using more cups (1 to 20) and/or more pennies.

Tangrams

Materials:

> Sets of tangrams
>
> Answer key for square, trapezoid, butterfly, and whale (see pages 101-102)
>
> Scissors
>
> Card stock

Helpful Hints:

> Use sets of tangrams that are different colors to help keep sets organized.
>
> Place answer key in a folder or envelope labeled "Answers" so participants can try the tasks before looking at the answers.

Math Standards in Action:

> Working with *Tangrams* helps students recognize and characterize geometric shapes and properties. Similarities and differences among shapes can be identified as students construct shapes and figures with the tangram pieces. Investigating how to put together and take apart shapes is important in early geometry.

Tangrams

Directions:

1. **Explore with a set of tangrams. There are seven pieces in a set of tangrams (two large triangles, two small triangles, one medium triangle, one square, and one non-square parallelogram).**

2. **Compare, contrast, and describe the shapes in the tangram set. Try making a large square using all seven pieces.**

3. **Try making other shapes, such as a large trapezoid. Try making figures such as a butterfly or a whale. These shapes and figures are in the "Answers" folder/envelope.**

4. **Record the information in your math journal.**

Questions Parents Can Ask:

How many ways can you make a rectangle using all or some of the tangram pieces?

What other shapes can you make?

Challenge:

Trace the pieces and make your own set of tangrams.

Geoboard Shapes

Materials:

Geoboards
Geobands (colored rubber bands)

Helpful Hints:

Display several geoboards to allow students and parents to compare shapes.

Math Standards in Action:

The *Geoboard Shapes* activity helps students to recognize, construct, describe, and analyze geometric shapes. Each shape that is formed can be described and compared in terms of the number of sides and angles. As they represent various geometric shapes, young students use spatial sense to visualize and recognize shapes from various perspectives. Specifically, they understand that a particular shape is still that shape regardless of its size, location, or orientation.

Geoboard Shapes

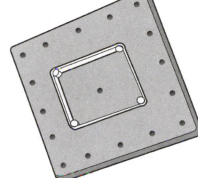

Directions:

1. Use the geobands to make shapes on the geoboard.

2. Try making shapes of different sizes.

3. Try making rectangles (including squares) of different sizes.

4. Try making triangles of different sizes.

5. Record some of your shapes in your math journal.

Questions Parents Can Ask:

How many pins does your rectangle touch?

How many different kinds of triangles can you make?

Can you make a circle? Why or why not?

Challenge:

Try seeing how many smaller squares can fit inside a larger square.

My Shoes

Materials:

Connecting links (sometimes called chain links)

Helpful Hints:

Avoid placing too many links at this station.
Participants only need to measure the length
of their shoes or arm lengths (challenge).

Math Standards in Action:

My Shoes is an activity that invites students to
explore with measurement using nonstandard
units. By comparing and ordering objects, students
further their understandings of the attributes associated with length. Students gain experience with
the procedures and descriptions associated with
measurement when they use nonstandard units
to determine the length of objects.

My Shoes

Directions:

1. Take off your shoes.

2. Measure the length of your shoe using connecting links.

3. Remember, length involves one side not the entire perimeter (around the shoe).

4. Do you think that your other shoe is the same length? Measure to verify.

5. Record the length of your shoe(s) in your math journal. For example, "My shoe is eight links long."

6. Compare and order several different shoe lengths.

Questions Parents Can Ask:

How many links long is your shoe?

How long do you think my shoe is?

How many links longer/shorter is my shoe than your shoe?

Challenge:

Measure the length of your arm using links. Compare this length to the length of your shoe.

How Much Will It Hold?

Materials:

> Bucket of uncooked rice
> Containers of various sizes
> Towel

Helpful Hints:

> If rice falls on the floor, it can cause people to slip and fall. Place a broom and dustpan by this station. Placing a towel under the bucket of rice helps with potential spills.

> To help students develop understandings about conservation, include some containers that hold equal amounts but look different. For example, tall, thin containers and short, wide containers.

Math Standards in Action:

> *How Much Will It Hold?* is an activity that helps students develop conservation skills as they work with measurement. Young students need many experiences with comparing and contrasting the capacity associated with various containers. These experiences serve as prerequisite skills for later work with volume.

How Much Will It Hold?

Directions:

1. Choose two containers.

2. Predict which container will hold the most.

3. Fill that container with rice.

4. Pour the rice from the full container into the comparison container.

5. Discuss and/or record the results.

Questions Parents Can Ask:

Which container holds the least? How do you know?

If the rice overflows, what does that tell us about the sizes of the containers?

Which containers hold the same amount of rice?

Challenge:

Try three or more containers.

Order several containers by predicted capacity.

Graphing Color Cubes

Materials:

> One-inch cubes of various colors
> Paper bag
> Crayons
> One-inch grid paper (see page 103)
> Scissors
> Glue sticks

Helpful Hints:

> Create and display a model graph so that students and parents understand how the final product may look. Be sure to include titles and labels.

Math Standards in Action:

> *Graphing Color Cubes* is an activity that highlights data analysis and probability. It is important for students to learn how to collect, organize, analyze, and interpret data. To do so, students sort and classify objects according to specific attributes. The representation of the sorting and classifying comes in the form of a graphic organizer, which in this activity is a bar graph. Probability is an integrated math concept in this activity as students predict which color will most likely be chosen next from the bag.

Graphing Color Cubes

Directions:

1. Place some cubes in the bag. Note how many of each color are placed in the bag.

2. Predict which color is most likely to be chosen. Without looking in the bag, choose one cube out of the bag. Place this cube on the grid paper.

3. Continue predicting and choosing cubes from the bag one at a time. Each time a cube is pulled out, place it on the grid paper to form a bar graph. Compare and contrast the data (information).

4. After all the cubes are out of the bag, describe the values of the categories associated with each section (bar) of the graph.

5. Transfer the information to the grid by coloring the corresponding grid boxes. Add a title and labels to your bar graph. Cut out your bar graph and glue it in your math journal.

Questions Parents Can Ask:

How are the color cubes represented?

How do the sorted cubes resemble a bar graph?

Which color is more likely to be chosen next? Why?

Challenge:

Try making a circle graph with the data collected.

Chapter Three:
Intermediate Stations

(Third Through Fifth Grades)

Magic Squares

Which Place is Best?

Hooray Array

Multiply on the Fly

Money Toss

Money is the Key

Clothesline Fractions

Fruit Salad

A Handful of Handshakes

Fun with the Greedy Triangle

Geo Goes Home

The Curse of Measurement

Honeybees

Pentominoes

My Spinners

Magic Squares

Materials:

Sets of dominoes

Helpful Hints:

Making a magic square is more challenging using only one set of dominoes because the possibilities are limited.

If available, use sets of dominoes that are different colors to help keep sets organized.

Math Standards in Action:

Magic Squares is an activity that provides students with a problem-solving experience as they work with numbers, ways of representing numbers, and addition. As students create the magic square they gain experience with equivalent representations of whole numbers. Additionally, students utilize meaningful strategies as they compose (put together) and decompose (break apart) numbers.

Magic Squares

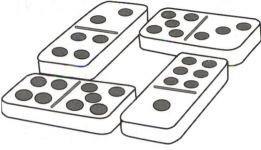

Directions:

1. A magic square uses four dominoes.

2. Each side of the square totals the magic number.

3. A magic 10 square could look like the one on the right.

4. Try making a magic 10 square in a different way.

5. Record your magic square in your math journal.

Questions Parents Can Ask:

*Which dominoes will fit into our magic square?

*Can we replace some dominoes and still make our magic square?

*What strategy are you using to complete the magic square?

Challenge:

Try making a magic 12 square. Try other magic squares.

Which Place is Best?

Materials:

> Place value frames (see page 104)
> Number cubes (dice)
> Overhead markers and wipes (optional)

Helpful Hints:

Provide multiple copies of place value frames.

If place value frames are mounted and laminated, players can use overhead markers to write on them and then erase the frames for multiple use.

Math Standards in Action:

Which Place is Best? helps students to develop a more complete understanding of place value. Using their knowledge of the base 10 number system, students generate, read, and compare six-digit numbers. An additional math concept in this activity is the probability of rolling specific digits on a number cube.

Which Place is Best?

Directions:

1. Each player uses her/his own place value frame.

2. Roll the number cube and write the number in any one of your six sections. The other player also writes the number in any one of her/his six sections (not necessarily the same section because each player may strategize differently).

3. Continue taking turns rolling the number cube and writing the digits until all of the sections are filled.

4. Compare the numbers created. The player with the largest value wins the round. Remember to read the number. For example, the number 634,152 is read as "six hundred thirty-four thousand, one hundred fifty-two."

5. Play three rounds.

Questions Parents Can Ask:

*Why did you place the digit there?

*What are the chances of rolling a six?

Challenge:

Try playing to get the lowest score.

Hooray Array

Materials:

Connecting cubes (multilinks or snap cubes)

Helpful Hints:

Display examples of arrays.

Math Standards in Action:

Hooray Array is an activity that encourages students to investigate the characteristics of numbers and operations in a hands-on manner. Students explore the meanings of multiplication and division, as well as how these operations are related.

Hooray Array

Directions:

1. Gather twenty-four cubes.

2. Make an array by connecting the twenty-four cubes into a filled rectangle (rectangular prism).

3. Discuss the number of rows and how many cubes are in each row.

4. Make all the possible arrays with the twenty-four cubes. List all the factors of twenty-four.

Questions Parents Can Ask:

What does a two-by-twelve array look like?

How many rows of six can you make with twenty-four cubes?

What other arrays can you make?

Challenge:

Make arrays with other numbers.

Try making a square array.

Multiply on the Fly

Materials:

> Number cubes (dice)
> Large box lid or deep tray
> Dry erase boards or chalkboards (optional)
> Markers, erasers, chalk (optional)

Helpful Hints:

Participants can write equations in math journals or on small dry erase boards or chalkboards.

The box lid or tray provides a contained area for the rolling of the number cubes (dice). If noise is a concern, line the lid or tray with a towel.

Math Standards in Action:

Multiply on the Fly creates an opportunity for students to engage in rapid multiplication of whole numbers. Students recognize and apply properties of operations, and they work with the associative and commutative properties of multiplication.

Multiply on the Fly

Directions:

1. One person rolls three number cubes into the box lid or tray.

2. All players write the multiplication equation on a board or in math journals. For example, 3 x 2 x 5 = 30

3. The first person with an accurate equation receives ten points.

4. All other players with an accurate equation receive five points.

5. Play continues until someone reaches 100 total points.

Questions Parents Can Ask:

What was the multiplication strategy that you used?

If you change the order of the factors will you still get the same product?

What is the highest/lowest product possible each time the three number cubes are rolled?

Challenge:

Try this activity using five number cubes.

Money Toss

Materials:

Money Toss posters (see model on page 105)
Beanbag
Play money (coins)

Helpful Hints:

Make the Money Toss posters before Family
Math Night.

Use the additional tool on page 105 as a model for
the Money Toss poster, or create your own.

Place the Money Toss poster on the floor to make
the "tossing" easier and more exciting.

Math Standards in Action:

Money Toss is an activity that encourages students
to develop fluency in adding, multiplying, and
estimating. Students recognize and apply strategies
used to compute monetary values. Additionally,
students are given the opportunity to enhance
estimating abilities.

Money Toss

Directions:

1. Take turns tossing the beanbag. Each player has seven turns. Estimate the total you will have after seven tosses.

2. Collect the money after each toss.

3. Keep a running total of the amount of money for each player.

4. Record the total and the estimate in your math journal.

Questions Parents Can Ask:

How much money do you have?

How much more/less do you have than I have?

How many different ways can we show five dollars?

Challenge:

Try playing the game using double scores.

Money is the Key

Materials:

Play money (coins and bills)
Number cubes (dice)
Money Key (see page 106)
Pretend checks (see page 107)

Helpful Hints:

Provide enough pretend money (particularly quarters, half-dollars, and one-dollar bills).

Use different colored number cubes for the challenge.

Math Standards in Action:

Money is the Key allows students to gain further knowledge and experience in understanding the base 10 system and computation. Because money typically proves highly motivating, students will be actively engaged in generating sums represented in various ways.

Money is the Key

Directions:

1. Each player rolls the number cube and collects money.

2. The Money Key indicates how much money the players receive for each roll.

3. Take turns rolling the number cube and collecting money. Compare the total amount each player has after each roll.

4. After ten rolls, exchange coins and bills as necessary. For example, exchange eight quarters for two one-dollar bills.

5. The player with the greatest amount receives a check for that amount.

Questions Parents Can Ask:

Who has more/less money?

What is the difference in the amounts?

How many times do you think you would need to roll the number cube to reach fifty dollars?

Challenge:

Roll two number cubes. One number cube tells the amount, and the other number cube tells how many times that amount you receive for the turn. Make a different Money Key and play again.

Clothesline Fractions

Materials:

    Index cards
    Clothesline (or thick string)
    Clothespins
    Markers
    Number cubes (dice)

Helpful Hints:

Hang the clothesline in a safe, secure location (against a wall is recommended).

Place a few index card fractions (for example, 1/3 and 2/4) in the correct order on the clothesline to help start the activity.

Math Standards in Action:

Clothesline Fractions **is an activity that allows students to explore the relationships among fractions. Using the clothesline as a number line, students compare and order numbers less than and greater than one. Specifically, students are recognizing, comparing, and ordering fractions according to relative size.**

Clothesline Fractions

Directions:

1. Roll two number cubes. Decide which number will be the numerator and which number will be the denominator.

2. Use a marker to write the fraction on an index card.

3. Use a clothespin to hang the fraction card on the clothesline (which serves as a number line).

4. Take turns rolling number cubes, writing fractions, and hanging the cards on the number line.

5. Continue until each person has placed four cards.

6. Make sure the placement and spacing of the fraction cards are accurate and draw the number line in your math journal.

Questions Parents Can Ask:

Which fraction has the greatest value?

How do you know where to place the fraction card?

How could you display equivalent fractions?

Challenge:

Try using four number cubes. Add two numbers to find the numerator and add two numbers to find the denominator.

Fruit Salad

Materials:

Sets of small plastic fruit or counters
Fruit Salad recipe cards (see page 108)

Helpful Hints:

If counters are substituted for fruit, use corresponding colors (red for apples, blue for blueberries, orange for oranges, and yellow for bananas) to help students keep track of information.

Math Standards in Action:

Fruit Salad is an activity that invites students to engage in early algebra. Students are analyzing mathematical relationships and solving unknown variables. While investigating how to create each fruit salad, students are using models, expressions, and equations to examine mathematical relationships.

Fruit Salad

Directions:

1. Pick a Fruit Salad recipe card to try.

2. Gather some plastic fruit or counters and try making the salad.

3. Illustrate your salad in your math journal.

4. Explain how you decided which fruits were in your salad. Use words, expressions, and equations in your explanations.

Questions Parents Can Ask:

What information is the most obvious?

Which clue helped you the most?

Is there another way to make the same salad?

Challenge:

Make a salad and write a recipe for someone else to follow.

A Handful of Handshakes

Materials:

Manipulatives to represent the people in the
story problem

Helpful Hints:

Post possible diagrams or lists that could be used
to solve this type of problem. For example, if there
were four people at the party the diagram may
include four circles with lines drawn from each,
representing the four people and the six handshakes.

Math Standards in Action:

A Handful of Handshakes presents an algebra
problem that encourages students to represent
problem situations through diagrams, lists, and
models. Students organize and analyze information
to find and explain the solution.

A Handful of Handshakes

Directions:

1. Draw a diagram, make a list, or use a model to find the answer.

EIGHT PEOPLE MEET AT A PARTY. EVERYONE SHAKES HANDS <u>ONCE</u> WITH EVERY OTHER PERSON. HOW MANY HANDSHAKES WILL THERE BE?

2. Explain the strategy you used to solve this problem.

Questions Parents Can Ask:

*How can you keep track of who has and who has not shaken hands?

*What strategy are you using?

*What if there were only six people at the party?

Challenge:

Try different amounts of people at the party. Look for patterns that will help you predict the number of handshakes.

Fun with the Greedy Triangle

Materials:

> *The Greedy Triangle* by Marilyn Burns
> Flex straws

Helpful Hints:

> Have plenty of straws available.

> Place a trash bin nearby.

Math Standards in Action:

> *Fun with the Greedy Triangle* is an activity that allows students to work with geometry. Students create, describe, modify, and classify shapes and attributes using geometric properties and mathematical vocabulary.

Fun with the Greedy Triangle

Directions:

1. Use flex straws to make a triangle. Connect the straws by pinching one end of the straw and placing it into another straw.

2. As *The Greedy Triangle* is read, add more straws to your original triangle to change the shape.

3. Use math words to describe and discuss the shapes.

Questions Parents Can Ask:

*How many sides does a pentagon have?

*Do all the sides have to be the same size?

*Which shape has eight sides? Does the shape name make sense? Why or why not?

Challenge:

Try making an undecagon and a dodecagon. Check the back of the book for definitions.

Geo Goes Home

Materials:
> Geo figure (see page 109)
> Spinner (see page 109)
> Geo grid (see page 110)
> Paper clip
> Number cubes (dice)

Helpful Hints:

Make Geo out of card stock, tagboard, or tiles and have several available for Family Math Night. Be sure Geo's figure is accurately duplicated on the front and back.

To use the spinner, place the paper clip in the center. Place pencil point through the paper clip at the center of the spinner. Holding the pencil securely with one hand, spin the paper clip with the other hand. If students are unfamiliar with this process, you may need to demonstrate how to use the spinner.

Math Standards in Action:

Geo Goes Home is an activity that invites students to investigate geometric transformations. Recognizing and demonstrating flips (reflections), slides (translations), and turns (rotations) are part of the study of geometry. Specifically, students are working with aspects of line and rotational symmetry.

Geo Goes Home

Directions:

1. Talk about flips, slides, and turns. In this activity:

    Flip is the reflection of a figure.

    Slide is the figure positioned (translated) one unit away.

    Turn is the figure rotated one unit (a 90-degree turn).

2. Each player uses her/his own Geo and grid.

3. Place Geo in the start position. Take turns spinning the spinner to find out if Geo will flip, slide or turn. Record Geo's position by drawing his face in the square after each move.

4. The winner is the first player to get Geo "home."

Questions Parents Can Ask:

Should you flip up, down, right, or left?

What will Geo look like after a turn?

Challenge:

Try playing using a number cube to roll the number of flips, slides, or turns. How does your strategy change?

The Curse of Measurement

Materials:

Math Curse by Jon Scieszka and Lane Smith
Math book with customary measurement chart
Measuring tools (quarts, pints, rulers, yardsticks)

Helpful Hints:

A math book with a measurement chart needs to be available for students who may need to check measurement relationships. If the information is not known by students, it is important that they know how to look up the information using various resources.

Math Standards in Action:

The Curse of Measurement is an activity that invites students to reflect on how math is everywhere! The humorous manner in which the authors of the book present mathematical ideas is engaging. The specific measurement activity encourages students to think about the relationships among units of measure by conducting simple unit conversions.

The Curse of Measurement

Directions:

1. Read *Math Curse* by Jon Scieszka and Lane Smith.

2. Discuss the measurement ideas and questions on page 5.

   Quarts in a gallon
   Pints in a quart
   Inches in a foot
   Yards in a neighborhood
   Inches in a pint
   Feet in my shoes

3. Write a letter in your math journal to the main character explaining your answers.

Questions Parents Can Ask:

   Which questions can be answered?

   How do you know or how can you find the answers?

   Which questions cannot be answered? Why not?

Challenge:

Explain real-life math situations you experience.

Honeybees

Materials:

Pattern blocks

Helpful Hints:

Post definitions of area and perimeter.

Math Standards in Action:

Honeybees is an activity that encourages students to work with measurement as they explore area and perimeter. Students use strategies for estimating and measuring the area and perimeter of various configurations. This activity helps students develop an understanding of the relationships associated with various areas and perimeters.

Honeybees

Directions:

1. The hives of honeybees are made up of many cells. Each cell is in the shape of a hexagon.

2. Using the pattern blocks, each person constructs a hive that is made up of fifteen cells.

3. Find the area (consider one hexagon as one unit) and find the perimeter (consider one side of the hexagon as one unit).

4. Compare the hives. If the areas are equal, will the perimeters also be equal?

5. Try making a fifteen-cell hive with the largest/ smallest perimeter.

Questions Parents Can Ask:

Which hive has the greatest perimeter? Why?

How can we make a hive with a smaller perimeter?

Is it possible to make a symmetrical hive?

Challenge:

Try making and comparing hives with a larger/ smaller number of cells.

Pentominoes

Materials:

> Square tiles
> Graph paper
> Scissors
> Answer key (see page 111)
> Folder or envelope

Helpful Hints:

> Display at least one of the pentominoes as an example.
>
> Post definitions of congruency, area, and perimeter.
>
> Place the answer key in a folder or envelope labeled "Answers" so that participants try constructing several different pentominoes before looking at answers.

Math Standards in Action:

> *Pentominoes* is an activity that helps students to develop richer understandings of how to measure area and perimeter. Students explore various techniques for measuring as they construct different pentominoes.

Pentominoes

Directions:

1. Make a pentomino by grouping five squares together so that every square has at least one of its sides in common with at least one side of another square.

2. One example of a pentomino is a rectangle formed by lining up all five squares. Try making more complex pentominoes (such as a "T" form). There are twelve different pentominoes.

    Note: If the pentominoes are congruent (same shape flipped or rotated), they are not considered different.

3. Draw your pentominoes on graph paper and cut them out.

Questions Parents Can Ask:

How do you know that you have made a different pentomino?

Do all of the pentominoes have the same area? Do all of the pentominoes have the same perimeter?

Which pentominoes can be folded to make a cube without a lid?

Challenge:

Try using all twelve pentominoes to construct a six-by-ten rectangle.

My Spinners

Materials:

Spinner templates (see page 112)

Small paper clips

Graph paper

Crayons or markers

Scissors

Glue sticks

Helpful Hints:

Display a sample spinner and graph.

Provide plenty of the spinner templates.

To use the spinner, place the paper clip in the center. Place pencil point through the paper clip at the center of the spinner. Holding the pencil securely with one hand, spin the paper clip with the other hand. If students are unfamiliar with this process, you may need to demonstrate how to use the spinner.

Math Standards in Action:

My Spinners is an activity that allows students to explore data analysis and probability. Students are collecting, organizing, and analyzing data from the spinner experiment. Students are also using what they know about probability to make predictions about the outcomes of the investigation.

My Spinners

Directions:

1. **Use the blank spinners to design two different spinners by coloring sections.**

   Note: Some sections can be the same color.

2. **If you spin each spinner ten times, think about the likely outcomes. Record these predictions in your math journal.**

3. **Spin each spinner ten times and record the outcomes. How do these outcomes compare to your predictions?**

4. **Use graph paper to make a graph of the results. Cut out the graph and glue it in your math journal.**

Questions Parents Can Ask:

Which color is most likely?

What are the outcomes of the investigation?

If you spin both spinners at once, what are all of the possible combinations?

Challenge:

Convert the outcomes to percentages.

Chapter Four: General Stations

(Prekindergarten Through Fifth Grade)

Let's Build Odd & Even Sums

Cereal Chains

Mancala is an Old Favorite

Can Family

Pattern Block Pictures

Just a Minute

How Long for a Kiss?

Red Hot and Ice Cold

Bubbles Bubbles

Don't Pig Out

Let's Build Odd & Even Sums

Materials:

Number cubes (dice)
Connecting cubes or squares

Helpful Hints:

Have plenty of connecting cubes available.
Display a few models of numbers.

Math Standards in Action:

Let's Build Odd & Even Sums is an activity that promotes hands-on experience with understanding numbers and ways to represent numbers. By using models to characterize odd and even numbers, students develop concepts for understanding the mathematical relationships among numbers.

Let's Build Odd & Even Sums

Directions:

1. **Roll two number cubes. Use the cubes or squares to make a model of each number. Use a different color for each number model.**

2. **Describe each number as odd or even.**

3. **Add the numbers together by joining the models.**

4. **Describe the process. For example, odd + even = odd. Is this always true?**

5. **Record the number sentence (equation) in your math journal. Draw pictures of the models.**

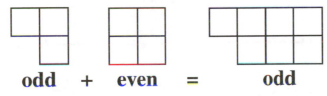

odd   +   even   =   odd

Questions Parents Can Ask:

*What does the shape of an odd number or even number look like?

*What kind of number do you get when you add two odd numbers? What kind of number do you get when you add two even numbers?

Challenge:

Roll four number cubes. Add four numbers or read the number cubes as two-digit numbers. Try adding odd and even numbers. Do the patterns change?

Cereal Chains

Materials:

> String/yarn
> Scissors
> Cereal (oat loops and color loops)
> Number cubes (dice)

Helpful Hints:

> Use child-size scissors or precut the string/yarn for this activity.

Math Standards in Action:

> *Cereal Chains* is an activity that invites students to increase their understanding of number and number relationships. By identifying specific numbers as more than or less than other numbers, students gain further knowledge about the relative size and magnitude of numbers.

Cereal Chains

Directions:

1. Each person takes a piece of string.

2. Take turns rolling the number cube.

3. If you roll a number that is less than 4, string an oat cereal loop.

4. If you roll a number that is more than 3, string a color cereal loop.

5. After you have played several rounds tie the string together and wear your cereal chain.

6. Compare and contrast the chains.

Questions Parents Can Ask:

If you roll 5, which cereal should you put on the string?

Who rolled more numbers that were greater than 3? How do you know?

What would the chain look like if you rolled 1, 2, 1, 2, 1, 2, 1, 2, 1, 2?

Challenge:

Try stringing oat cereal loops for even numbers and color cereal loops for odd numbers.

Mancala is an Old Favorite

Materials:

Mancala board
48 stones

Helpful Hints:

The Mancala board has six "bins" on each side and one larger "Mancala" bin on each end. The Mancala board can be purchased at toy stores or it can be made using an empty egg carton. The lid from the egg carton is cut in half and placed under the egg carton to serve as the larger "Mancala" bins on each end. Counters or glass gems can be used as the stones. Glass gems are often available at craft/dollar stores.

Math Standards in Action:

At a very basic level, *Mancala is an Old Favorite* is an activity that serves to help students to increase one-to-one correspondence. At a higher level, *Mancala is an Old Favorite* encourages students to use what they know about numbers and number combinations to strategize. Deciding which bin of stones to sow involves making mathematical decisions and predictions. Students are problem solving as they develop number sense.

Mancala is an Old Favorite

Directions:

1. Two players compete to try to accumulate as many stones as possible before the other player clears her/his side of the board.

2. To begin the game, place four stones in each bin. Each player has a "home" bin (called the Mancala) at the right end of the board and a side of bins to try to clear.

3. The first player picks up all stones in any one of her/his bins. The player then "sows" the stones by placing one stone in each bin to the right (including Mancala bins).

4. If the last stone is placed in the player's Mancala, she/he can go again. If the last stone is placed in any other bin, it is then the other player's turn. However, if the last stone is placed in an empty bin on the player's side, she/he captures all the stones in the opponent's bin that is directly across from the empty bin. Captured stones are placed in the player's Mancala.

5. Play continues until a player empties all the bins on her/his side. The winner is the player who has the most stones in her/his Mancala.

Note: Mancala is an ancient African game. Some historians believe Mancala was the first game ever played.

Questions Parents Can Ask:

Which bin of stones should you sow? Why?

What strategy did you use? How did your strategy help you?

Challenge:

Begin with only two stones in each bin.

Can Family

Materials:

Two-pan balances
Cans (film canisters and lids with letter and name labels)
Various amounts of sand or pennies inside can

Helpful Hints:

Use six or more film canisters as "cans" to represent the people in the Can family. Label each can with a letter and name. For example: A-Alonzo, B-Brittney, C-Cate, D-Derick, E-Ebony, and F-Frank. Fill each container with a different amount of sand or pennies. Make two cans (C and D) the same weight to represent the "twins" in the Can family.

This activity works best if cans are centered at equal distances from the center of the balance.

Math Standards in Action:

Can Family is an activity that encourages students to work with algebra. To understand how to represent and analyze numeric structures, students need to grasp the concept of equality associated with algebra. This activity allows students to use objects to represent values as they form simple equations and expressions. While investigating algebra, students are also using concepts associated with measurement of weight.

Can Family

Directions:

1. Pretend the cans are people in the Can family.

2. Without opening the cans, put the people in order by weight. Use the two-pan balance.

3. Try to find the twins in the family.
   Hint: Two Cans weigh the same amount.

4. Try placing more than one Can in one or more pans to create a "balanced equation." Does A + D = E?

   Note: Consider the arrangement of the cans when creating a balanced equation. To accurately portray the equation, the cans must be placed at equal distances from the center of the balance.

5. Create several algebraic equations. Record your findings in your math journal.

Questions Parents Can Ask:

*Which two Cans are equal to one Can?

*If you add Cate to one side and Derick to the other side, do you still have a balanced equation? Why or why not?

Challenge:

Assign numeric values to each member of the Can family.

The border of the page repeats the equation: $x = y + \bigcirc$

Pattern Block Pictures

Materials:

Pattern blocks

Pattern Block Names Chart (see page 113)

Helpful Hints:

Display the chart of shape names.

Post definition of symmetry.

Encourage participants to use the shape names (hexagon, trapezoid, parallelogram, rhombus, square, and triangle).

Math Standards in Action:

Pattern Block Pictures is an activity that helps students to recognize and characterize geometric shapes, properties, and transformations. Similarities and differences among shapes can be identified as students construct figures and designs with the pattern blocks. The use of geometry vocabulary is a critical element in constructing math knowledge.

Pattern Block Pictures

Directions:

1. **Explore with the pattern blocks.**

2. **Create a pattern block picture. Try making a flower, windmill, person, or other design.**

3. **Refer to the Pattern Block Names Chart to discuss the shapes used in your picture.**

4. **Draw one of the pictures in your math journal.**

Questions Parents Can Ask:

How many red trapezoids did you use?

How many green triangles cover a yellow hexagon?

Does your picture have symmetry? Why or why not?

Challenge:

Try giving values to the blocks and finding the total value for your picture.

Just a Minute

Materials:

> Stopwatches
> List of tasks (see page 114)
> Dominoes
> Bubble gum
> Paper and crayons
> Number cubes (dice)
> Trash bin

Helpful Hints:

> Have sugar-free bubble gum available.
>
> Place a trash bin nearby.
>
> Depending on the brand of the stopwatch, directions for how to "reset" may need to be available.

Math Standards in Action:

Just a Minute is an activity that promotes measurement in the area of time. Students need to develop a conceptual framework of how long certain tasks take in order to understand how time is measured. By estimating and verifying time, students improve their understandings of this abstract mathematical concept.

Just a Minute

Directions:

1. **Read the list of tasks. Decide which task you would like to test.**

2. **Estimate how long it will take you to perform the task. Record your estimate.**

3. **Ask someone to keep track of the time.**

4. **Perform the task. Record the actual time.**

5. **Compare your estimate to the actual time. Did you make a good estimate?**

   Note: A good estimate is in a close range, not necessarily the exact number. While some estimates are better than others, an estimate can never be wrong.

Questions Parents Can Ask:

*Which task will probably take the longest?

*Were you surprised by any results?

*How close is your estimate to the actual time?

Challenge:

Do you spend more time getting ready for bed or getting ready for school? Why?

How Long for a Kiss?

Materials:

Chocolate candy kisses
Stopwatches
Trash bin

Helpful Hints:

Replenish the supply with extra chocolate candy kisses as needed.

Place a trash bin nearby.

Depending on the brand of the stopwatch, directions for how to "reset" may need to be available.

Math Standards in Action:

How Long for a Kiss? is an activity that encourages students to work with time measurements. Because time is often a difficult concept for students to understand, increasing the amusement and frequency of experiences with time is helpful. By estimating and verifying time, students strengthen their conceptual frameworks about time.

How Long for a Kiss?

Directions:

1. Choose someone to keep the time.

2. Estimate how long it will take you to eat a chocolate candy kiss.

3. Start the stopwatch and eat the chocolate candy kiss.

4. Stop the stopwatch and record the time.

5. Compare the actual time to the estimated time. Discuss appropriate estimation ranges.

Note: A good estimate is in a close range, not necessarily the exact number. While some estimates are better than others, an estimate can never be wrong.

Questions Parents Can Ask:

Do you think you could eat another chocolate candy kiss in more time/less time?

How long do you think it would take you to eat three chocolate candy kisses?

Challenge:

How long will it take you to eat a chocolate candy kiss while singing one of your favorite songs?

Red Hot and Ice Cold

Materials:

> **Thermometers**
> **Cups**
> **Water**
> **Pitcher of ice**
> **Hot pot with water**
> **Towel**
> **Paper towels**

Helpful Hints:

> **Keep the hot pot in a place where it can be monitored.**
>
> **Use a safe temperature for the water. Add warmer water to the cups of water occasionally.**
>
> **Place towel under the cups of water in case of spills.**

Math Standards in Action:

> *Red Hot and Ice Cold* **is an activity that invites students to work with measurement of temperature. Students need to build understandings of the measurable characteristics of objects, such as temperature. Knowing how to use the measurement tool (thermometer) and knowing the appropriate units of measure (degrees) are important mathematical abilities.**

Red Hot and Ice Cold

Directions:

1. Examine a thermometer.

2. Discuss the number sequence and skip counting on the thermometer.

3. Find the red line indicator.

4. Put the thermometer in a cup of ice or water.

5. Discuss and/or record the temperature changes.

Questions Parents Can Ask:

*What happens to the red line indicator when the thermometer is placed in warm water?

*Which cup has the warmest water? How do you know?

*What is the actual temperature?

Challenge:

Try predicting and recording the temperature of the water in each cup.

Bubbles Bubbles

Materials:

> **Bubbles and bubble blowers**
> **Paper towels**
> **Trash bins**

Helpful Hints:

> **Use small bottles of bubbles. Refill bottles as needed.**

> **Place trash bins nearby.**

Math Standards in Action:

Bubbles Bubbles **is an activity that encourages students to work with data analysis. Students collect data as they count and record the number of bubbles. The data are organized and displayed in the form of a table. By asking and answering questions about the data, students are engaging in data analysis.**

Bubbles Bubbles

Directions:

1. **Make a table in your math journal**
   Example:

Name	Turn #1	Turn #2	Turn #3	Total
John	14	23	18	55
Mom	17			

2. **Each person will blow bubbles three times.**

3. **Record the data and find the totals.**

Questions Parents Can Ask:

*How many bubbles did you blow?

*Who has the greatest total?

*Looking at the data collected so far, how many bubbles do you think you will blow next?

Challenge:

Try estimating the total number of bubbles in four turns.

Don't Pig Out

Materials:

Number cubes (dice)
Note cards (optional)

Helpful Hints:

Some students may want to write their totals on note cards. Other students may want to record totals in their math journals.

Math Standards in Action:

Don't Pig Out is an activity that helps students to understand probability. The theoretical probability of a number cube labeled 1-6 involves a 1/6 chance for any one of the six numbers. Considering this basic probability, students engage in making predictions about the likelihood of specific outcomes.

Don't Pig Out

Directions:

1. The goal is to be the first to accumulate a score of one hundred or more.

2. On your turn, roll two number cubes as many times as you like, mentally keeping a running total of the sum.

3. When you decide to stop rolling numbers, record your total for that round. As the game continues add each new score to the score of your previous rounds.

4. If a 3 comes up on one of the number cubes, the player's turn ends and zero is scored for that round. If a 3 comes up on both number cubes, not only does the turn end, the total accumulated so far falls to zero!

Questions Parents Can Ask:

What is the probability of rolling a 3?

What is the degree of likelihood of rolling two 3s?

How likely is it to roll without a 3 coming up?

Why do you think this game is called Don't Pig Out?

   Hint: Pig has three letters.

Challenge:

Try using three number cubes.

Chapter Five:
Additional Tools

Family Math Night Invitation to Parents

Family Math Night Journal Cover

Family Math Night Evaluation Form

Try to Go Home

Let's Go to the Bank

Tangrams

Graphing Color Cubes

Which Place is Best?

Money Toss

Money is the Key

Fruit Salad

Geo Goes Home

Pentominoes

My Spinners

Pattern Block Pictures

Just a Minute

Family Math Night:
Math Standards in Action

You are Invited to Family Math Night!

On _____ (date and time)

_____ (school name)

will hold an exciting event called Family Math Night! Students, parents, siblings, and other relatives are invited to attend a fun-filled evening of mathematical pleasure. The intent of Family Math Night is to participate in math standards in action as we strengthen the mathematical application, problem solving, and communication skills of students through the power of family interaction.

We encourage you to continue to support your child's mathematical growth through your participation in Family Math Night.

Family Math Night at _____
School Name

_____
Date

Family Math Night:
Math Standards in Action
MATH JOURNAL

Student's Name: _____

Family Math Night:
Math Standards in Action

_____
(School Name)

_____
(Date)

Did you enjoy the Family Math Night?

Which activity did you like the best?

Which activity do you plan to try again at home?

Would you change anything about Family Math Night?

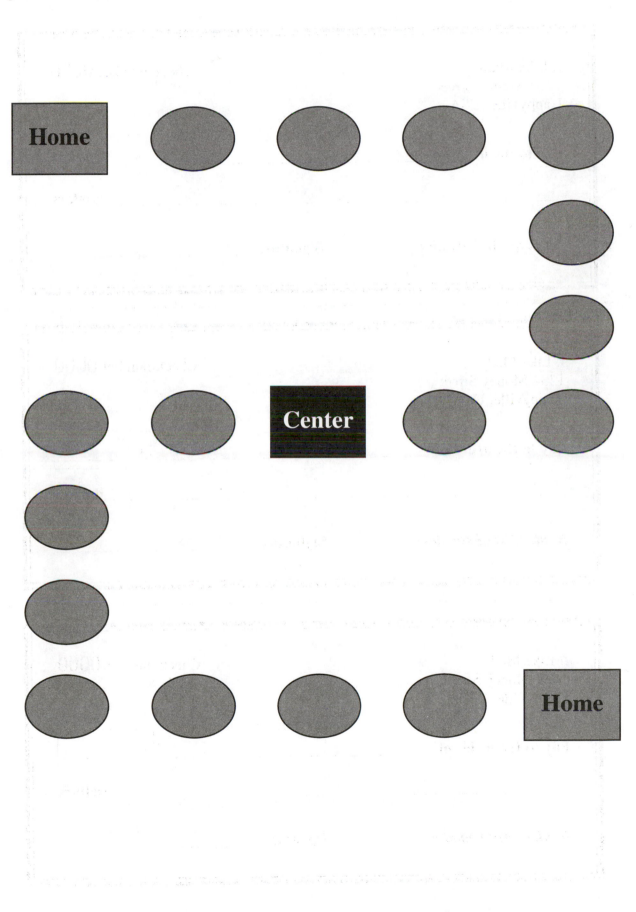

I. Like Math
1234 Money Street
Happyville, USA

Check number 0000

Pay to the order of _____ $ _____

_____**dollars**

Bank of Mathematics

Signature _____

I. Like Math
1234 Money Street
Happyville, USA

Check number 0000

Pay to the order of _____ $ _____

_____**dollars**

Bank of Mathematics

Signature _____

I. Like Math
1234 Money Street
Happyville, USA

Check number 0000

Pay to the order of _____ $ _____

_____**dollars**

Bank of Mathematics

Signature _____

Square

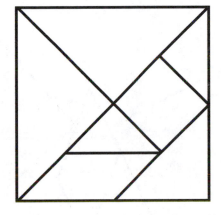

Trapezoid

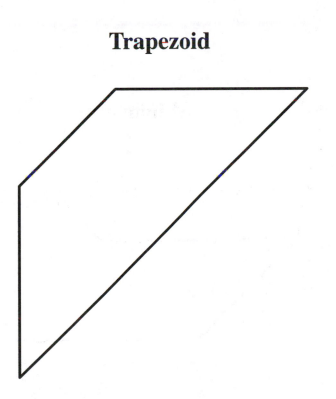

Butterfly

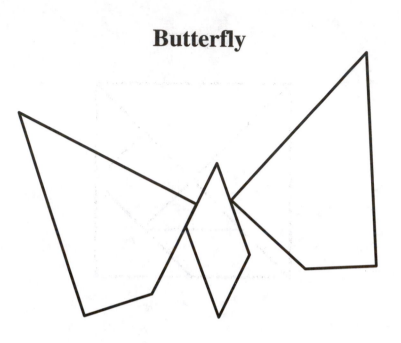

Whale

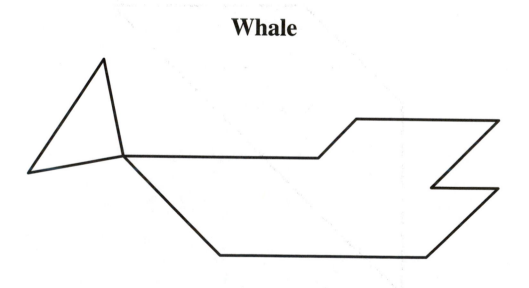

Graphing Color Cubes

Which Place is Best?

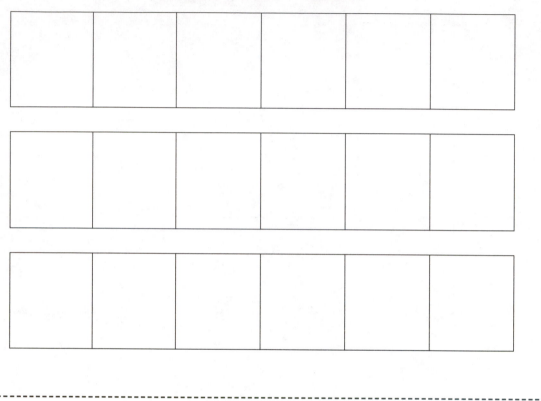

✂ -

Which Place is Best?

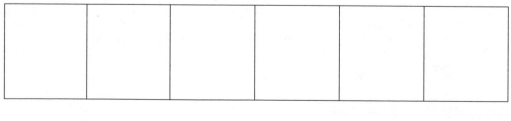

12 dimes	**18 cents**	**1 quarter**
4 pennies	**50 cents**	**9 nickels**
20 dimes	**2 cents**	**3 quarters**

Money Key

1	**$1.00**
2	**$1.50**
3	**$2.00**
4	**$2.50**
5	**$3.00**
6	**$3.50**

Money is the Key

Dollars N. Cents
100 Math Rocks Avenue
Bucksville, USA

Check number 0000

Pay to the order of _____ $ _____

_____ **dollars**

Bank of Mathematics

Signature _____

Dollars N. Cents
100 Math Rocks Avenue
Bucksville, USA

Check number 0000

Pay to the order of _____ $ _____

_____ **dollars**

Bank of Mathematics

Signature _____

Dollars N. Cents
100 Math Rocks Avenue
Bucksville, USA

Check number 0000

Pay to the order of _____ $ _____

_____ **dollars**

Bank of Mathematics

Signature _____

Sweet Fruit Salad

11 fruits altogether
3 apples
Twice as many oranges as apples
Some grapes

Tropical Fruit Salad

14 fruits altogether
5 cherries
1/2 as many bananas as oranges

Delicious Fruit Salad

12 fruits altogether
1/4 of the salad is made of strawberries
There are 1/2 as many grapes as bananas
There are some blueberries

Geo

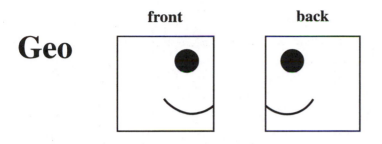

front   back

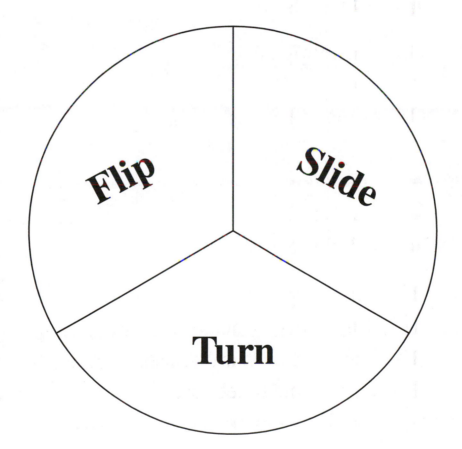

Start					
					Home

Pentominoes: Answer Key

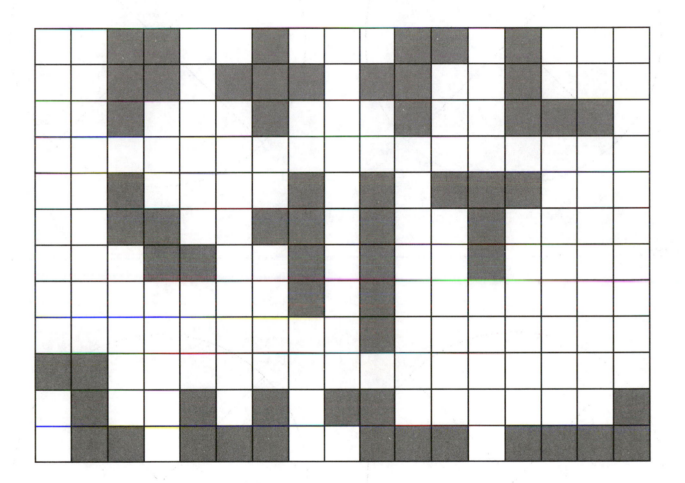

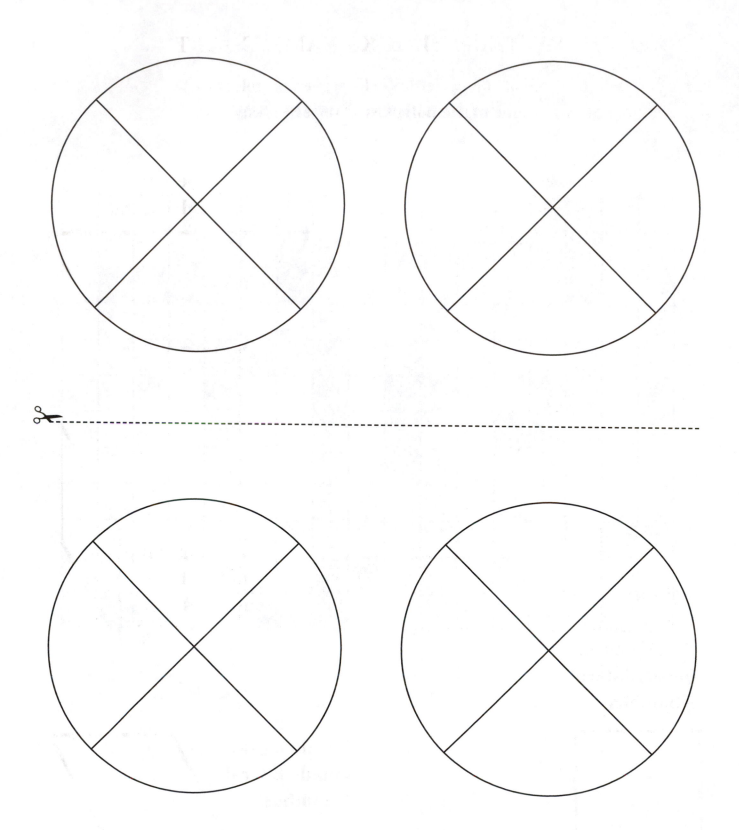

PATTERN BLOCKS NAME CHART

**All of the pattern blocks represent polygons.
Some of the polygons have several names.**

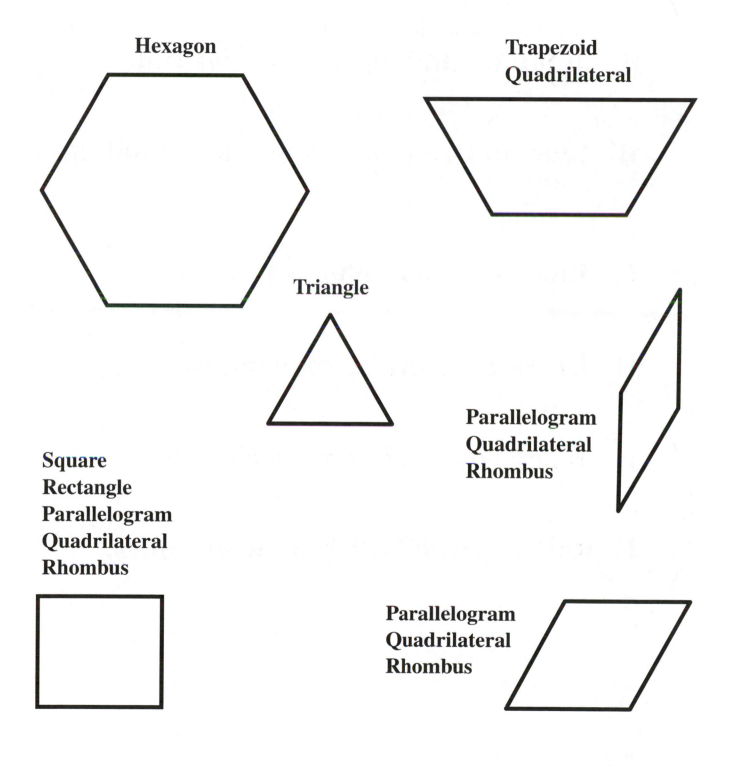

Hexagon

**Trapezoid
Quadrilateral**

Triangle

**Parallelogram
Quadrilateral
Rhombus**

**Square
Rectangle
Parallelogram
Quadrilateral
Rhombus**

**Parallelogram
Quadrilateral
Rhombus**

Just a Minute List of Tasks

A. Jump up and down sixty-five times.

B. Line up twelve dominoes in a standing row.

C. Blow a large bubble with gum.

D. Draw a picture of your family.

E. Write your full name backwards.

F. Roll a "seven" using number cubes.

Notes

Notes

Notes

Notes

Notes

Notes